82ND DIVISION

D.M. ADERIBIGBE

NATIONAL POETRY SERIES WINNER
SELECTED BY COLIN CHANNER

BROOKLYN, NEW YORK
Publishing books since 1997

The National Poetry Series congratulates the five winners of the 2024 National Poetry Series competition:

Our Hands Hold Violence by Kieron Walquist
Chosen by Brenda Hillman for Beacon Press

82nd Division by D.M. Aderibigbe
Chosen by Colin Channer for Akashic Books

Blue Loop by AJ White
Chosen by Chelsea Dingman for University of Georgia Press

Games for Children by Keith Wilson
Chosen by Rosalie Moffett for Milkweed Editions

Shade Is a Place by MaKshya Tolbert
Chosen by Maggie Millner for Penguin

The National Poetry Series was established in 1978 to ensure the publication of five collections of poetry annually through five participating publishers. The series is funded by the Academy of American Poets/Amazon Literary Partnership, William Geoffrey Beattie, the Gettinger Family Foundation, Bruce Gibney, the Tabitha and Stephen King Foundation, Anna and Olafur Olafsson, Penguin Random House, the Poetry Foundation, the Gil Schwartz Foundation, and the National Poetry Series Board of Directors.

———

Published by Akashic Books

ISBN: 978-1-63614-242-5
Library of Congress Control Number: 2025933491

First printing

Akashic Books
Brooklyn, New York
Instagram, X, Facebook: AkashicBooks
info@akashicbooks.com
www.akashicbooks.com

EU Authorized Representative details:
Easy Access System Europe
Mustamäe tee 50, 10621
Tallinn, Estonia
gpsr.request@easproject.com

Table of Contents

Introduction
by Colin Channer

When I first read the work that forms this book, I was struck by the ways in which myth, magic, and music work with and against each other on the level of the line. In short, I was wooed by a poetic intelligence, namely Aderibigbe's sense of material and its engagement through the kind of tensile curiosity readers experience as lyric force. There is something ancient in Aderibigbe's lyric awareness, but something futurish as well, the two combining with the present in ways that transfix, recalling what happens when a lute or oud is noted in the music of today. Casually metaphoric, Aderibigbe moves through his landscapes while uttering in argots of prophecy, his pitch a microtone above the everyday, thus gettable at gut bottom, but dreamily a bittish out of reach, leaving room for our ascending. It's transcendent, this book, this gift from this observant itinerant, this wandering mind.

Like most people who write poetry, I am not so good at it. What I am good at is sticking with a draft till it goes from not-good to something better, ideally without the effort of the making sweating through. As such, I have a deep respect for poetry that comes with some nickmarks of its fashioning when done. I am not speaking here of craft, though craft is a part of it. I am speaking more of the deep humanness—the line's terror and the greater terror of facing the self as subject in ways that take in wider views, allowing one to peer at one's own persona from odd angles, knowing all vantages do not provide good looks. The nickmarks I speak of are the ones remaining from personal, societywide, and politico-historical violence, and the hurt that comes from having to apportion this in a continuum from everyday rough-up all the way to abuse. And how tender must a poet be to work this, make loveliness and love from all this? And how tough too? For it takes a hugeness of spirit to crawl back through the lines to see again what occurred in that household, in that school, in that Englishness as language, the lines cutting the scout again and again, the mind acting like the barbs are buds.

Aderibigbe is an unsentimental but tender poet, one willing to revisit the scenes of crisis to ruminate, to re-comprehend, to sacralize, be jubilant, and—in the most accomplished poems in this most stunning work—to give elegy. In elegy, Aderibigbe is huge in compassion and/but ruthless in cutlassing untruth—the blood of false emotion a reminder that suffering is the cloud-mess of particulates we live in, and that simply to have it gasp us, or for us to cry-cough it, does not make what comes out because of it art.

The elegy is one of the most difficult frames and forms for many of the now-er poets to work in/with. It's old-timey, sort of, and maybe a bit too comfy in adjacence to prayer in what are not god-look-to times. Plus, making elegy also asks a lot from/of poets, as some of the best examples of the form are conjured not for the dead and their survivors only, but also for the deepest poetself.

As proven in poem after poem, D.M. Aderibigbe is an especially capacious poet, one given to take on/in more ache than he perhaps deserves—more ache, more grief, more loss, more verdigris regret, distinguishing himself by his ability to root elegies not just in sorrow, but also adventitiously in forgiveness, absolving. Big poets know they stunt their own growth as humans by disguising elegizing as redress.

Part of the pleasure of reading Aderibigbe is the artisanal nature of the craft in/of his poem-making and the questions his poems evoke surrounding the evolution of his poetself. Idiosyncratic, his language stands out, especially in America, where the sound of poetry has plateaued, sort of, or more generously, prairied, flattened notably, glad, it seems, to be unriddimic, content to be mind-read and not said aloud. There is a certain kind of privilege that assumes each reader can afford their own book; a peculiar version which cannot, or does not want to, imagine what it means to be from or live in a country where poetry and music are, if not twins, the children close in age of the same loose dad. Aderibigbe has something that has glorified the poetry of greats, including Dawes, Szymborska, Heaney, and Khoury-Ghata—a regard for "thingness" . . . an awareness of the sonics brought into a poem by details, especially in the form of nouns, the proper names of things, but also the feel for how the poem is the sibling of cinema, how they share the freedom of quick cuts, juxtaposing, how they cooperatize to think imagistically, how they taproot in something ancient, that which gave us magic, music, myth.

It is a distinguished and distinguishing pleasure for me to write these words of appreciation and honor to/for a poet who has, through work, talent, sense of material, and again talent, arrived at a place of serious consideration in the imagination of American poetry. Nigerian by birth, Aderibigbe is America homed now, and seems poised to inflect our understanding of the world and ourselves from an angle that will only make our self-reflection more complex. In saying "our," I am reminded I have not always been "here" and that the openness of American poetry has been a boon to others and me. It has been said that America's self-denial of the truth of its enduring postcolonial anxieties has at times allowed its poetry to relax into the arms of small concerns. The expression often used is "intimate." In less generous moments I describe it as poems made to mumble to the self. The poet as public figure is still vibrant in other parts of the world, and with it comes the sense that poetry is oral always, even when written down. This sense of the poem as a creation made ear-first and eye-second is vital to a fuller appreciation of Aderibigbe's art. To read his lines aloud is to experience a flash of what it is to be a poem, voice cords strummed.

Colin Channer's most recent book is Console *(FSG, 2023) a* New Yorker *Best Book of the Year. It was also listed for the PEN/Voelcker Award. His other work includes* Providential *(Akashic Books, 2015), which was listed for the OCM Bocas Prize. A 2022–2023 Cullman Fellow at the New York Public Library, he was born in Jamaica and teaches at Brown University.*

Lagos

I stand in a nest of noise—
discordant danfo buses fill
the day's lungs.
On either side of me
stalls made out of plastic bags:
spinach, okra, bell peppers
on parade like national pride.

I come back to memories seeking shelter
from untamed sun:
a schoolboy sucks juice out of a finger
of sugarcane at a bus stop.
His friend, closely behind, dances
to Olamide's "Eni Duro" booming
out of a nearby barbershop.
In front of a face-me-I-face-you building,
a shriveled voice shreds a fable
for a party of teenage ears.

I stand in the land of lagoons
where sons of the soil became visitors
to their own visitors—
as local lore tells us.

Eko akete, ilu ogbon. Lagos,

the land of my mother, and her mother.
This land where whatever's left of me will shrink to dust.

1

Midnight Blues

The night beats itself against the door.
The night, a dogged bird, against the door.
O, the feral street, feet on the tip of my mind.

Outside, I stand in a circle of noise.
Outside, I sing in a circle of noise:
Fear's a fallen angel. O, ask the mind.

My muscular but quiet neighbor speaks.
My muscular neighbor, for once, speaks:
We tiptoe. Walk. Run. Stop. Sit quietly in some bush.
We tiptoe. Walk. Run. Stop. Sit quietly in some bush.

Sitting: strange voices afar.
Squinting: strange men afar—
the smoky remains of our homes aim for the night sky.

These days: every mass of smoke, a page of night sky.

Autobiography

By the papaya tree,
a dragonfly wandered under a green sky.

Nearby:
a tribe of tomatoes
and a family of fluted
pumpkin
leaves latched onto slices of sunlight for lunch,

cicadas covered all corners
of the afternoon with chorus.

In the shadow of the brick fence
next to my room's window:
midges converged, like an overcast,
above a leftover
of the previous night's rain,

a renowned rooster returned
for another
portion of my generosity.

On the balcony,
my mother and her sister
talked and toasted
over palm wine and fried fish.

A meter left,
my cousins ran, wildly,

from one end of the compound
to the other
like all
animals in their natural habitat.

This was before
the fire.

2

Failed Elegy

The gold chain sitting
on her outstretched palm
is a good place to start.
Her father—your grandfather—kept
it in a secret drawer for a day
like this—a day
you would have a piece of him
around your neck.

Your grandfather, in your mother's words,
refused to let his daughter
feed her present with the future.
And on the night that you were born,
he drove all the way from Benin to Abuja.
That night, silence became your mother.

All your life, you've only seen this woman
through your father's eyes.
Here, a story you longed for is telling
itself. Should you be grateful?
Should you think:
what does it matter that the first time
your mother kisses you on the cheek
she is standing on her toes?

Duplex (An Elegy Is)

An elegy is a love poem.
Says my uncle—who smiles into a mirror.

My uncle smiles into a mirror:
the face he worships is a palace.

The face he worships is a palace
of wrinkles—though, nothing new to see.

Lo ti to, wrinkles are nothing new to see:
time is a bus, always on the road.

I am a bus, always on the road:
old lovers now mistake me for a stranger.

My lover warns: don't make me a stranger,
love, if what we have were ever over.

Love, if what we have were ever over,
would we be an elegy or a love poem?

Rose

I came to my aunt
with a flower. For days,
she had lived on scraps of light
and the echoes of her own voice.

It was yellow—
yellow, the opposite of silence.
It was a dahlia, but she named it *Rose.*
Rose, not the flower,
but the Pomeranian she'd recently lost
to her feral imagination.

Isn't it a thing of wonder how life finds us?
my aunt said. And for a start,
she opened
                    her window
for morning to wander in.

A Brief History of My Grandmother

The hiss of a kerosene lamp,
the screech of the bed,
a dwindling light,
a menagerie of worn-out memories,
my grandmother's unfettered voice—
in this order, is how I remember
that night's beginning.

The room, an island
of army ants.
I climbed my grandmother's back—
she ferried me out.

In the backyard:
I sat, stared at the doorway
as she marched back
in with a pair of flaming rags.

Outside My Grandmother's House

I'm clearing wreckages left by a windy night. The task is mighty. Two younger boys are playing with bottle caps in front of an empty store. *The task is mighty,* I say to the boys. And with the prize of a twenty-naira note hoisted in the hot air like the Nigerian flag, the boys pledge their allegiance.

Deep into the work, the boys begin to argue: the older wants more of the money—for being older. The younger wants equal share—for doing as much. Right outside my grandmother's house,

history barks at itself.

The work done, the boys come to me, each still clinging to his side of the argument. I drop the prize in front of the empty store—

who am I to dictate to history?

Window

When I open the window,
a stretch of sunlight seeks survival
on the center table.

The other side:
two chubby children build their lives
with jollof rice and sparkling water.

A boy whose bones will rust in a few days
sitting alone, thinks and thinks—
hunger, such a righteous disease.

Hunger, such a righteous disease?
Sitting alone, thinks and thinks
a boy whose bones will rust in a few days.

With jollof rice and sparkling water
two chubby children build their lives.
The other side:

on the center table,
a stretch of sunlight seeks survival
when I open the window.

Pantoum

My father's hands were fluent as a boxer's.
The first time I saw them at work, I was barely six.
My mother had mouthed off a mild protest.
She couldn't use that mouth for days.

The next time I saw them at work, I was barely six:
that morning was heavy with noise.
My mother couldn't use her mouth for days.
Afterward, silence became her first language.

That morning was heavy with noise:
my mother had shrugged him off in mild protest,
since silence was her only language.
I think of her face—his hands, fluent as a boxer's.

Essay on Love

The last time I stepped out of her
gray hair, the town fell around my
grandmother's feet. It was the first day of high
school. A month before, we buried my mother.

Ritual

Each morning, I gather what's left of her—
a face towel, old and raggedy—
call this a son's ritual for his mother.

Call it an orphan's daily prayer.
Don't call this a triumph. Don't call it an elegy—
each morning, I gather. What's left of her,

I place, tenderly, on my shoulder
until the day wears itself out. Call this a journey.
Call this a son's ritual for his mother.

Emptiness fills every space in your heart, a lover
says, one night, while we're on the corridor of intimacy.
The next morning, I gather what's left of her—

my mother—dip it, like a piece of laundry, in water
and run it across my face. What would she
call this? A son's ritual for his mother

still? A declaration of love over
love? I call this a journey.
Each morning, I gather what's left of her.
Call this a son's ritual for his mother.

English

There are eight people in my family, only one speaks English.
I was born with Yoruba, at thirteen I came to English.

Before my tongue's baptism, I was tied
to silence; I'd learned the stupid speak Yoruba, the smart, English.

Once, a boy from my new school denied
his mother to me because she knew no word in English.

Grandma bought me my first dictionary the day I came home to hide
an old raggedy textbook called *New Practical English.*

On mother's proud days, I was the dictionary on which she relied—
D.M., a name I found, shortly after her death, through English.

3

Morning Devotion

We kneel before metaphors:

our hands clasped,

eyes, the opposite

of the chapel's beaming lights.

We kneel until

we hear the chaplain's bell.

We hear the chaplain's bell

and gather outside to gather

unholy things:

sheets of paper orphaned the night before,
bits of bread bearing bite marks,
trampled bottles,
chewed chewing gum,
strands and strands of hair . . .

We wipe sweat off
our faces with muddy hands.

Good job so far, boys, the matron says, in her
customary thunderous tone.
As you know:
cleanliness is next to holiness.

Haibun: Annual Manual Labor Day

There's a green field inside the matron's steely gaze. Instead of sweeping through it with a machete like your peers, you sit on the other end of the school compound, among a constellation of short shadows, and pick out peanuts from your protruding pocket. Around you, a stretch of tall grass bends to the tunes of the afternoon breeze, chickens bathe in warm sand, and lizards of all stripes seek crickets to crush.

You have been here before.

You know too well that, soon enough, you will hear the footsteps of the past year at your doorstep. You know too well that, soon enough, the night will birth another blood-soaked memory.

Night returns early
in December—that cool warmth,
those sonorous snores.

Lunch Break

On the field ahead,
a loud kitten lay
still as a fallen tree branch—

his forelegs shackled
with strands of carelessness.

I'd never held a cat in my hand.
But like him, I too hope

someone will disentangle me
from loneliness

someday—when they hear my cry.
I'd hardly worked
through the hairy puzzle

around his legs
when he began to push

them against my palm.
Finished—I dropped him on the ground:

his legs free
of hair, but not of the bloodied legacies
it had left on them. He pushed

against the ground—rose—
but could barely beat a second
before going down again.

I left for class.
He was gone when I returned.

I still wonder what happened to him.

The Origin of Fear

There is my favorite senior boy
holding on to the evening's
garment; his girlfriend refused

to let him step his dirty feet
back into her life.
So he wet his flaming

intestine with a small bottle
of insecticide.
The matron is squeezing

those feet now. And the head nurse,
pouring all of her knowledge—syrups,
capsules—into his withering mouth.

Then there is me, trying to close
my eyes. Because of him,
the night is scared to arrive.

New Year's Eve

The year's last child is on fire—
the street watches.

A girl pulls a boy
from time's prison.

They begin to search
for silence—their first

(which they soon find
under a papaya tree).

They rest on the trunk of their wish.
She asks him to close his eyes—

a story begins.

Duplex (I Will Tell You)

I will tell you all about desire.
One night, a man picked up his bag and walked.

One night, my father picked up his bag and walked.
His big brother became the story.

My big brother once told a story,
he ended up choking on a stroke of joy.

If rightly stroked, would you choke on joy?
So asked my last girlfriend in high school.

I asked my last girlfriend about high school
memories—she's a genius in disguise.

Memories are geniuses in disguise:
love without faith is lost, my wife once told me.

Love without faith is lust. My wife once told me:
oko mi, what do you know of desire?

Suleja

My last name fills the air
like a piece of rare music.

My father—at the doorway
to the principal's office, arms folded
across chest, gaze guzzling
the sky—walks
left to right,
right to left,
like a man
hustling for divine intervention.

His once charcoal-colored afro,
now a swath of gray grasses.
His face, wrinkled
by long absence.

He pulls me close
with his right hand.

Gba mi gbo,
my memory is wild
as a blackbird in the sun:

more than once, I saw my mother's blood
coat that hand.

That's all I could think about.

Origin of Faith

We diluted our prayers with yawns:
morning clothed in darkness
and cold. At every sound of the bell
in the chaplain's hand,
we were quiet
as a house in mourning.
Soon a man—the matron's man—
barged into our silence:
screaming, running
across the chapel. He knelt
at the feet of a statue of Jesus—
Christ's feet, soaked
in liquid agony!
The chaplain jingled
the bell: we lined
out of the chapel
as a funeral procession.
Because curiosity was my religion,
                                        I slipped out of the line.

I crawled behind the matron's
window—looked:
a body covered with a piece
of clothing, the color of day,

lay on a table. Olu, the matron's
only son, stood close,
covering it with whispers.
The whispers soon took the shape of prayer—
the prayer, the shape of whispers.

The Teacher

For Mr. Chukwuma

The silver cross
pendant sparkling
from his chest is what remains:

but before now,
he moved everything he owned—
a wardrobe of shiny shoes,
a room of stylish shirts and polished pants,
and a fairly new Volkswagen Jetta—
out of his father's luxurious shadow.

He sold everything he owned
for a one-way ticket to Rome.
I must be the first Black pope.
That's the dream—everything he owned.
He slept on several sidewalks of his dream
for a year. He slept on several sidewalks,
for a year, after the dream.

    Back home—

            he took to teaching.

GATHERED DURING A SCHOOL TRIP TO THE OLD COLONIAL SECRETARIAT, LAGOS

*   *   *

At first they sought to stuff the local chiefs'
heads with all sorts of gifts.

*   *   *

I'll say, at your age, you all should know
the language your history speaks.

*   *   *

In Berlin
between 1884–85, tension

about how to share Africa
was examined and settled

among warring European nations.
And it was determined:

each nation hoisted its flag
on any African land

in their line of sight.

That way, a territory was drawn.

*　　　　　*　　　　　*

Sir, sir, is this how the British flooded our history?

4

I

Christening: An Abecedarian

Aframomum. Black-eyed bean. Cocoa bean.
Buried—in sacks—in the cargo hold.
Columbite. Gold. Pegmatite. Tantalite.
Dragged onto the lower decks.
Every single day, a crowded ship sailed
from the coast of Lagos to Bristol.
Grenade. Gun. Gun. Gun. Gun. Gunpowder. Gut.
How did anyone think we made the Africans dig
in the sun, sow in the rain, reap in the sun?
Joining each man was his wife and children—
kids, old enough to walk, joined in.
Later, each man, under the control of another
man, controlled his family to fill the sacks.
Nigeria. Sudan. West African Guinea.
Of all names that swam to the bank of my mind (I had the
pleasure of coming up with the names), these three,
quite frankly, stood out like stars. For a
real estate property, any of those names
sounds about fine. In the end, I settled for
the one I coined last—"Nigeria." *Bible. Mirror.*
Umbrella. Vase. We arrived bearing gifts, knowing
very well what they wanted—what we wanted.
We arrived sharing gifts, knowing what we wanted—killing

xenophobia, top on the list. For a full

year, we did this. Then we attacked: *Lion. Lioness.*

Zeal. Zeal. Zebra. Zebra. Zebra. Zebra. Zilch.

Notes:
Flora Shaw, a British woman, suggested the name "Nigeria" for the British colonialists because the term was shorter and thus a better fit for a real estate property in place of the previous Royal Niger Company territories (Kwasi Kwarteng, *Ghosts of Empire: Britain's Legacies in the Modern World* (PublicAffairs, 2012)).

An Explanation of Colonialism

I

That evening still burns.
In truth, fire had no place in the plan,
neither did Maxim guns. I placed no man
in the town, and asked them for no returns

—nothing—from their trade.
What happens when patience gets tired?
Well, the lone thing my pocket desired—
removing a new-build blockade;

allowing my men
move materials to the colony
from the north—the town's king turned down. Money?
A visit from the best of my men?

Personal letter
from the Queen? Gifts of mirrors, compasses,
toothbrushes, fans, and wineglasses?
What, in the Queen's name, didn't I offer?

II

Before I floated my first offer,
before the first fire ascended,
before bullets were born. Men, higher
in rank than all but the Queen, visited

a town lying north of my future.
The men arrived with a journal filled
with manifold intentions: a culture
where beings kowtowed to things—beings, thrilled

to jump into the same river they drank,
beings eating with bare hands while sitting
on dusty ground—needed, to be frank,
to be purified. Without wasting

the Lord's time, the men moved around
like news—touching every door and backyard.
Teaching every man and woman they found.
Then came the town's king, then came his guards.

III

Soon came the town's king. Soon came his guards
wielding cutlasses, knives, stones, and shards
of rocks. My men, dragged to the town square.
It was the time of day when God's stare

was fiercest. *Look, Africa belongs*
to Africans; I will dance to no songs
by the white man. None. Tell your commanding
officer I said so. Said the town's king.

Did he not know that I would always fight
for every land that came to light?
That my God, in his prodigious glory,
always granted me victory?

The day was barely alive when I led
men out of the colony: a thread
of moving field caps. We, with two concerns,
reached the town. Gunshots. Fire. It still burns.

Notes:
In 1892, the British attacked Ijebuland using Maxim guns. The attack fulfilled two purposes: one, it helped them create a freeway between the colonies in the south and north for movement of goods and services. Secondly, it helped them achieve complete dominance in the southwest area surrounding Lagos, the seat of the colony.

A Brief History of Pride

1. Homecoming

Father's dearest, raised
on nan's raisin and kidney pie,
I have returned home to you with a sky
of bronzes. Brass face

masks, ivory tusks, tin,
and wood carvings, in legions, also trailed
me home. Soon, the Queen's medal, which I failed
to wear with my kin

five years ago, will shine
from my chest like a mirror in summer.
From the podium, I will watch each drummer
attempt to align

themselves with a trumpeter:
music is born. The Queen and I motion
in an ocean of high and low keys—ocean
of teeth and *thanks*. Her

hands gesture: a golden gun
drawn on the sun—a gang of shots;
the type that greet great men who just earn their spots.
I made us proud, son.

2. Kingdom

When I was seven, my brother
and I found ourselves on the shores
of beauty, through a book our mother
brought. The book tells of a kingdom around
the Benin River: one whose doors
are made of gold, ground

made of tin, and water made of oil—
shrines stuffed with bronzes and ceramics.
Like other kingdoms that share the soil
of Africa, the ones here are unfit
to lead themselves—the dynamics
of governance, the wit

to outlive challenges, the flair
to manage resources, elude
them. Son, as lights of the world, we bear
the responsibility of leading
these benighted lot out of their crude
ways to a cultured living.

3. Battlefield

News spread like an airborne disease:
British forces brought to their knees
  by Benin's border guards—
which is a clement means to say
Britain was bettered in a way
  that showed that the right cards

were played by the Africans. The Queen's
agony had two heads: Blacks, with genes
  as impoverished as dogs'
should not be winning any combat,
only if clumsiness was the heart
  and soul of their foes. Like hogs,

the British forces were slaughtered
for sheer rashness! The Queen's eyes watered
  when she thought about it:
if only General Phillips
waited for consent, the last of his trips
  would not be the last—would it?

4. Departure

I had just buried myself
in the year's first sun,
when, from the Queen herself,
a message arrived: I must burn
down all breath, turn

day to night, bread to stones
in the kingdom of Benin.
The king must be hanged. The bronze
plaques and sculptures, oil, rubber, tin,
and everything

else must become ours. Lesson
must be learned: no Blacks
who attacked us lived to sin
another time. These were clear facts
of life—all acts

of disrespect have wages,
as stated in our Holy
Book. We boarded ships in stages:
from Gold Coast, son, we sailed proudly
toward glory.

Notes:
On January 4, 1897, the British, led by Acting Consul General James Robert Phillips, attempted to seize the West African coastal kingdom of Benin, but were defeated by the kingdom's guards. Eight days later, the British, under Rear Admiral Harry Rawson, led an army from nearby Gold Coast to Benin on a punitive expedition. The kingdom was burned to the ground, with the British looting its tin, rubber, bronze statues, and much of its art (which is displayed in British museums to this day).

II

After a School Trip to the National Museum of Colonial History, Aba

After an image of soldiers from different parts of Africa fighting alongside the British in Burma in 1942.

There are the binoculars which sit
on the tilted face of the only
British man in the photograph.
There are the African *soldiers*, seven of them,
who look to him like a savior.
He stands in a shield
made of their bodies. Two blocks

of blackened air split
the entire field into three
columns—each dark column a paragraph
of fallen men, of motionless mayhem.
The man's thumb seems set to rise—again—to spur
the African *soldiers* on this battlefield
to fire—again—what each clutches: a paradox.

82nd Division

September 1943

I sit on the last row of my mind—
the day finally lodging in my calves.
At every turn of thought, I see
all that still breathes in my past: my wife,
our twin toddlers, our blooming dahlias.
At every turn of thought, I see
that sunny day: while whistling my way
through the garden I tended—
each of my palms a bed of blisters—
three men, British, barged into my view,
two grabbed me by my underpants. The third—
the man who owned the garden—stood beside them.
At every turn of thought, I hear
his words: *He'll be useful. He knows English.*

September 1943

His first words to me: *Be useful—teach them English*
or at the very least, interpret their duties.
Commander Bruce is a man of few words.
Before the words come the boots. Before the words
always come the boots, as we found out

that night, our first night. In truth, we failed
shooting tests, failed to finish
building a fort or cleaning up the base. We failed
to understand that we could not sleep
until the commander's words had come to pass.
In truth, it was our first night on land in a week.
While we slept, leather feet, large and small—
and sizes between—traveled from our chest to toes.
Our bodies, signs of a bruised future.

September 1943
My bruises, signs of a future
that awaits, should I deviate
from the rules; it was my work
that every Black man knew a new
English word each day. It was my work
that every Black man fell in love
with the battlefield. It was my work
that every Black man's dusk and daybreak
were born from the mouth of the general.
It was my work that every Black man ended
every sentence with "sir." It was my work
not to call white lies, lies. I was handed
a pair of journals and ink. I slipped
out a spare, with which I write right now.

September 1943

There is no spare time to write. Right now
I should be sleeping—it's one for the other.
But as Chidi, my closest friend
here, always says: it's only fair
that history remembers the sound of our voice.
He was in his living room, about to eat
dinner with his wife and three daughters,
when some feet tore through his front door.
Among us, there are as many children as parents:
look at Tade, thin as a lizard's tail.
He had just got out of school—
his first day of high school—when
a colony of colonial officials
swarmed and shoved him into a waiting van.

June 1944

They swarmed and shoved me into a waiting hole,
the British soldiers. Since that night,
I've stopped raising my voice on the battlefield
to any of the boys who fails to discern
an enemy's trap—whose feet make

a deathly choice. Our British superiors,
riding on armored tanks behind,
never mention these traps either, leading
the hazy ground to furiously feed
on our boys. In fact, days before that night,
Commander Bruce pulled me into his tent—
that day he called our dead *necessary bait.*
That day he vowed to drown me in sand
when next my voice rose on the battlefield.

December 1944

Smoke rose from their bodies on the battlefield
—our newly dead. Many of them arrived
here in Burma about two months ago.
Their first night in camp, they revealed their journey:
as though they just came out of a coma—
they woke to themselves on a ship sailing.
Taken from their babies' babblings, wives' kisses,
mothers' wrapped arms. Fists on their faces
or stomachs—last lights in their memories.
They woke to themselves on a ship sailing.
In Kenya, they scaled trees, hid, shot—for four years—
till the war was won. The war won—surviving
men shoved on a ship sailing for Ceylon.
Fought there for five months—then to Burma they sailed.

April 1945

Fought for nineteen months—soon, from Burma our ship sails.
Bags strapped to back, I look back at tent
after tent—all now empty—and think of men
whose tales turned the nights blue. Men whose hums
sent our part of camp into gyration.
Men whose songs have become mine—ours.
Men whose bones have become mine—ours.
Men whose eyes have become mine—ours.
The surviving few are among the crowd,
like me, waiting on the commander
to make his way to the podium.
Amid our British superiors'
ear-splitting cheers and chest pounding,
we—the African contingent—link our arms.

April 1945

We—the African contingent—link our arms
while the commander gives the victory
speech—sounds of clashing palms follow every sentence.
In his speech, he extends his gratitude
to the Queen and the prime minister.

In his speech, he extends his gratitude
to all the British soldiers who made
this victory a reality.
In his speech, he extends his gratitude
to British people everywhere.
In his speech, he extends no further gratitude.
Sounds of clashing palms follow. We follow
the British soldiers' order to the ship—
I sit in the first row—home on my mind.

Notes:
The 82nd (West Africa) Division was an all-Black army regiment made of personnel forcibly conscripted from various parts of Nigeria. The regiment was, in turn, part of over 3.5 million Africans who fought in the two world wars, resulting in 2.1 million African deaths (James Luto, *Fighting with the Fourteenth Army in Burma* (Pen & Sword Books, 2013)).

5

The Porter

Oh boy, the matter plenty,
but I go try cut am short.
You see dem marks for my face,
both the big one and small
small ones, and the other ones
for my body, wey you no fit see
because my clothes dey cover dem,
I get gem all for Burma when I
bin dey fight for the British.

Yes nau. Na bomb bin explode behind
me. Na God say I no go die, my pikin.
You see these marks, dem never heal for
over forty years. Every night, na so so
pain before I fit sleep. Even now, if I
touch dem, I go feel pain.

No be your fault, my pikin. No be
even the worst be that. When we
come back from that war, dem no give us
anything. Shishi we no see. Na why I
come dey do this security job, na.
Na the story be that oo. Thank
you say you listen oo.

Letter from My Father, Odysseus

Omo mi a ta ta, I do not need / to remind you of years / I spent on the edge / of disappearance / the many memories / made of your uncle's whips / are enough. Emi na mo, you must be wondering / why I keep bathing / my fingers in these wounds / from the past. For the past is where we are / now. As you read this, I would again be gone. / Gone like a precious stone / thrown in a river. Gone / like a name / sold into slavery. I would be gone. Gone. / Omo mi ata ta, rise each night, walk / through every gate. If they ask you where you are / going, tell them to fight a battle. Walk / until solitude fills / your fists. Fall / on your knees, make sure your vision is darker / than the darkness around. / Scream and scream until God's / ears begin to hurt.

The Looted Are Our Ancestors

In a display case in   museum in London

museum in New York

Stolen   stories

Identity,   history.

Objects of admiration   were objects

containing

information.

The artifacts—known as Benin Bronzes.

Notes:
An erasure poem based on the article "In the West, the Looted Bronzes Are Museum Pieces. In Nigeria, 'They Are Our Ancestors,'" *New York Times*, June 23, 2021.

Independence Day

This hour of the year in Suleja, the sun grows
cold, and the leaves of the dogonyaro tree
that mans the school's only field become shadows.
In this hour, students who are lucky
enough form a square in the center of
the field—each one's pair of arms taped to their body;
legs close enough to make their thighs kiss. Above
them, a green-white-green canopy.
On its left side, their parents, waving flags that bear
the canopy's color—zealously
singing: *Dis Nigeria na we own. No where*
fit dey like home . . . On the right side are the unlucky
students and their parents, looking on
shamefully, then shamelessly, then proudly,
while the principal rounds up his drawn-
out speech. The lucky students march, on the count of three.

Christmas in Suleja

All night, the kitchen stays awake:
Murmuring aromas stream out of a pot
of jollof rice; the scream of one bean cake

after another in burning oil; the quake
of a knife tearing chickens apart—hiss of the hot
water awaiting them. The TV stays awake

all night: *Ti Oluwa Ni Ile, Prison Break,*
The Adventures of Sir Lancelot,
Merlin, Ayọ Ni Mọ Fẹ, Cake:

A Wedding Story . . . At daybreak,
we wear our anticipation: tailor-made, store-bought.
All morning, our feet stay awake:

we serve neighbors near and far. Take
food to friends. Return plates to those who brought
us food. Some give money. Some, a piece of fruit cake,

for our joyous trouble. When, finally, we make
it home: a heap of grandma's steamed pride sits in an iron pot.
Surely, all year, this memory stays awake:
plates of jollof rice, chicken, bean cake . . .

6

Postcolonial Prayer

Lord, bless us with butterflies
in place of locusts,
chinaberry tree in place
                                        of yew.

Make all still cheeks take flight,

or,
            Lord,
give back our breaths.

Acknowledgments

"82nd Division" is after "Native Guard" by Natasha Trethewey.

"Duplex (An Elegy Is)" and "Duplex (I Will Tell You)" are duplexes—the duplex is a poetic form invented by Jericho Brown.

I'm grateful to the Mississippi Arts Commission, Sewanee Writers' Conference, and PEN America for the resources they provided at different stages of this project.

More than anything else, I'm grateful to God for the gift of poetry.

I'm grateful to Colin Channer for believing in this work and selecting it as a National Poetry Series winner.

I'm grateful to my professors at FSU, David Kirby, Barbara Hamby, James Kimbrell, Maxine Montgomery, and Frank Gunderson, whose feedback helped turn this book from a rough dissertation to what it is now.

I'm grateful to Pastors Taiwo Olarinde, Kayode Fakunle, and Joseph Akande for their prayers and spiritual guidance.

I'm grateful to the homie Saddiq Dzukogi, for his feedback and friendship.

I'm grateful to my family in Nigeria, the Aderibigbes, Adegbites, Oshos, Adenijis, Makanjus, and Akandes, for their prayers.

I'm grateful to my family in America, Siena, Jett, Ursa, Steve, and Jeryl Oristaglio (Mama O), for their ceaseless love and kindness.

Most importantly, I'm grateful to my son, Damilola, and my sweetheart, Shanoya, for always inspiring me.

Once again, I'm grateful to my sweetheart, Shanoya, for her invaluable feedback.

Grateful acknowledgment is made to the editors of the following journals in which versions of these poems have appeared or are forthcoming:

Atlantic: "Failed Elegy" published as "Heritage"
Callaloo: "Origin of Faith"
Hopkins Review: "Midnight Blues"
Hudson Review: "English"
Jubilat: "Origin of Fear"
Michigan Quarterly Review: "Window"
New England Review: "Christening: An Abecedarian"
North Dakota Quarterly: "New Year's Eve"
Ploughshares: "Duplex (I Will Tell You)"
Poetry Review: "Letter from My Father, Odysseus"
Shenandoah: "Duplex (An Elegy Is)"
Southern Review: "Lagos"